# COMMON SENSE IN TEACHING AND SUPERVISING

## A Practical Guide for Student Teachers and Student Teacher Supervisors

## Douglas M. Brooks

University of Texas at Arlington

UNIVERSITY
PRESS OF
AMERICA

LANHAM • NEW YORK • LONDON

To my teaching models, my students, and their students.

iii

Some debts can never be repaid. Ron
Dowell should consider this manuscript a
beginning.

# TABLE OF CONTENTS

1190 35

The first year that I taught children formally, I was asked to give the commencement address for the eighth grade class. The title of my address was "You can lock me in jail for a hundred years, but you can't keep my face from breaking out." The thrust of the speech was that experience is the best teacher, not always the most kind, but certainly the most effective. I argued that children need experiences and that to deprive them of experiences in the belief that we are sparing them grief is short sighted. This manuscript, like my speech, is an affirmation of experience. Much of what I have been taught has only added meaning and clarity to my early teaching and supervising experiences. I have been told by veteran teachers that what I say is common sense, hence the title, Common Sense in Teaching and Supervision.

Douglas M. Brooks
Arlington, Texas
1977

# INTRODUCTION

Part I is written for student teachers and first year teachers who are lying awake, terrified at the thought of being isolated in a classroom with thirty-five kids. The night before the first day is a time when anyone with words of advice becomes a friend for life.

The educational training system may crumble the night before you teach. The material in Introductory Educational Psychology courses has slipped from memory. How is all that stuff about learning theory going to help you survive tomorrow? Gone are the professors who told you of the excitement, challenge, and satisfaction of teaching. Gone is your supervising teacher and college supervisor. Both have had their phone numbers changed and didn't leave a forwarding address. Remember, you're reading this primer because you want comfort. You're having visions of nine foot students refusing to do anything you tell them.

But wait! You're sure the little hints you need will be in at least one of those twenty education books you still own. You hope they'll tell you exactly what to do if the nine footer says "No, I won't do it, and you can't make me."

The back of texts have a way of always letting you down. The authors never quite make the vocabulary shift that is necessary for comprehension under stress. And you are under stress! You don't want anything analytical. You don't want anything you have to outline. You know how tough it is to recall under stress. You don't have the advantage of experience. You need some-

thing you can say over and over and as you
drive to school. Does this help? "I'm going
to be firm and fair, firm and fair, firm and
fair."

How did that make you feel? Are you getting drowsy? Maybe you're even calming down
a lettle. Maybe now you won't run into the
room screaming, "I'm the teacher and you're
going to do exactly what I tell you to do!"

If repeating "I'm going to be firm and
fair" makes you feel any better, you might
want to keep reading. Not all the "hints"
included in this primer will be explained at
great length. You be the judge. If you find
yourself still reading when your alarm goes
off, maybe we've done some good for you and
for the kids you'll be with in thirty minutes.

One "hint" before the "hints". Stop
worrying about being the teacher. Think for
a minute about the teachers you liked. Why
did you like them? Probably it goes something
like this. He or she had expectations for you,
wanted you to do well and wanted to help you
succeed. The room was controlled. You can't
learn anything at a pep rally. And you felt
you could ask questions without feeling foolish. Imposed silence when you had a question
isn't a lot of fun.

Remember the teachers you didn't like.
Nobody likes a pushover and nobody likes a
dictator, so try not to sound or act like
either one. Nobody likes anybody that's too
nice too soon or too aloof too long. See,
it's just regular stuff.

Is it time to go to school yet? Remember the kids in your class are just as

nervous about meeting you as you are about meeting them.

    Read on!

## AFTER YOU'VE PARKED YOUR CAR

Don't go to the teachers lounge. You'll
just get teased about being new, as if you
had forgotten that you had been awake all night.
Don't worry. Nobody will notice the bags
under your eyes. Some of the teachers in the
lounge may be supportive but you won't remember them. Somebody will ask if you're nervous.
They can't tell you're sweating. You wore a
sport coat today. The fact that it's August
28, it's 100 in the shade and the air condi-
tioning isn't on in the building shouldn't
tip anybody off that your judgement has been
blurred by terror.

Try this. Pass by the office to let the
principal know he won't have thirty kids
tearing a room apart because the new teacher
is hiding in a locker. Go directly to your
classroom. Check it out. Do you have a
desk? Oh God, let there be a desk! Are there
plenty of chairs? It's not unlike a new teacher to fall prey to a more experienced teacher's
ability to accumulate chairs. Do you have
chalk? Do you have an eraser? If it has
blood on it, get back in your locker or run
for your car.

Newer schools might have other standard
classroom equipment. Overhead projectors are
very popular. Do you have the right kind of
pen for the overhead? Watching your lessons
dry up and disappear on an overhead may under-
mine your credibility. Do you have sunglasses?
Many teachers have suffered permanent retina
damage when they turned on an overhead pro-
jector while looking at their lesson plans on
a transparency. I'm kidding about the sunglasses. I'm also kidding about the retina
damage.

4

Instead of rushing into the classroom
and sitting behind your desk, go sit in a
kid's desk. Pick one in the back of the
room. Just sit there for a while and think
about being firm and fair. Think of the
difference between being firm and being auto-
cratic. Firmness is control with fairness.
Fairness is treating the kids the way you
wanted to be treated when you were in school.
Let yourself feel a sense of mission and
committment to a task. That's enough head
stuff. Now, here's why you're in your room
and not in the teachers lounge.

If you watch the kids come into your
homeroom or first class one at a time, they
won't scare you as much as if all thirty were
in the class and you walked in to greet them.
You've met many people individually. It's
only when you have to give a speech and meet
three million people in one second that your
mouth dries up. If you meet them individually,
you may not react to them as a group when you
talk to them. You may sound a little less
like a marine drill instructor if you aren't
frightened. Your voice won't crack and your
mouth won't dry out.

On the chance that your mouth does dry
out, in spite of "preventative introducing",
put a glass of water on your desk or in your
pocket. Line your pocket with a baggie.

Here's what you've accomplished so far.
You've gotten to school without being sick.
You've avoided the teachers lounge because
they'll tell you things you either don't want
to hear or already know. You've checked out
your room. You have what you need. You've
met kids a little more informally and you
have "firm and fair" etched on the back of

your hand with the overhead pen that quite obviously does work. The next sound you hear will be a bell.

# AFTER THE BELL RINGS

After everyone is seated (see why you check for enough chairs), there is usually some formal school stuff to do; items like attendance, head counting, etc. I would describe these items as "things-you-have-to-do-before-you-can-get-started-so-just-bear-with-me-for-a-while" stuff. Don't try to be innovative at this stage. Just do these tasks the way you remember having had it done to you. After one to eleven years in school, the kids know how to take attendance better than you do, anyway.

A lot of "sizing up" goes on the first day. But it's all happening in what could be described as a "momentary power vacuum". The kids may not know each other very well. Don't delude yourself into thinking they would rather get to know you than the first chair tuba player, last year's homecoming queen or Tony Touchdown. So what you do is kill two birds with one stone. You learn their names and in the process they learn each other's names. You help yourself and you help them. In the vacuum of unfamiliarity, you take control and let people find out a little about each other. This starts with learning their names.

Take a bunch of 3X5 cards. Pass them out or, better yet, have somebody in the back of the room pass them out. Kids in front always want to help. There's no challenge in asking them. Ask whoever is doing the passing what their name is and "would they help". It's a question that's not really a question. What are they going to say? "No, I won't." You haven't commanded them to "Pass these out." The word "would" is the difference between a command and a request. Firm and fair, remember?  If you've forgotten, it's on your hand.

Have them fill out the cards with their
name, plus any nickname they might have.
Imagine how ridiculous you would feel calling
Reggie Jackson "Reginald".  Get their home
address and phone.  You know why you want it.
They know why you want it.  You might ask for
their age, hobbies, kind of car they drive,
favorite subjects, etc.  When you've got the
cards back, move out from behind the desk
(it seems safe back there doesn't it?) and go
through the cards one at a time.  Maybe you
had a '53 Chevy, too!  What's all this card
business about?  You're a teacher not Monty
Hall.

Did you ever want a teacher to know your
name?  Not because of something good you did
like "Everybody, look at Marilyn's paper.
Why don't the rest of you write like she does".
But because you just wanted the teacher to
know who you were.  Students like to have
teachers know them.  A name is the beginning.
The 3X5 card is the way.  You can go through
the cards at the beginning of class, in the
middle or at the end.  Be sincere about learning what's on them.  It may take two weeks,
but you won't believe the problems you won't
have if you take the time to learn names.  In
P.E. classes, put names on tape and put the
tape on the front of T-shirts.

The reason you are nervous about the first
day is because it's important.  Learning a kid's
name says something to him or her about you.
Without having to say something dumb like "I
want you to like me, so you won't give me any
trouble", you're being friendly.  Besides, you
can talk to each other without wondering if
you know each other's name.

8

Have you ever talked to someone and been convinced they didn't remember your name? If you know a person's name, you use it. You can also stop many classroom disturbances sooner and more effectively if you know a specific name. Rather than saying something really personal like, "Hey you in the back of the room, quiet down"; try, "Bill can I see you after class?" The "hey you" method could refer to anybody in the class and very often you'll hear nine kids say, "Who me?". Predictably it's noisier than before you tried to quiet things down. Is it making sense? Keep reading!

## MRS. ANDERSON HAS SO MANY RULES

We've all been in classrooms where the teacher had made so many rules that only the brightest students could possibly remember them all. A classroom with hundreds of rules can be a scary place.

In these classrooms, not only are the children expected to remember the rules, but the teachers are required to remember them also. The less the children can remember, the more they will require the teacher to recall, enforce and arbitrate the classroom rules. The more rules you have in your classroom, the greater the probability that you will make errors of judgement. Your preoccupation with order through rules may turn you into a lawyer instead of a teacher.

Try this common sense approach to rule making: "We should probably talk a little about classroom rules. You all have a good idea of what appropriate and inappropriate classroom behavior is and so do I. My intention is to enforce common sense rules which you already know. The first and perhaps most fundamental rule is that when I am talking to thr group, I want you to listen. If I am talking, you listen and then when you talk, I will listen. If you listen, you will understand directions, etc. and that can only help you. If I am talking and I see someone else talking, that person is ignoring the one rule that is important to the entire class. It's simple courtesy. When we listen to each other all other expectations will fall into place."

Noise is situational. There are times when one level of noise is all right and other times when the same level of noise will bother

10

you.  The difference is between "busy noise"
and unproductive disorder.  Learn the difference and expect quiet when you feel it's
reasonable to have it.

What's nice about this rule is that it is
easy to enforce.  It's clear and simple.  It's
common sense.  It's a good first day rule.
This rule becomes the medium through which you
may establish yourself as the teacher.

## THE BELL ALWAYS RINGS WHEN THE
## SECOND HAND HITS THE FIVE

Picture for a moment a sophomore English
class that meets during fourth period.
Fourth period is like no other period.  Fourth
period is the one before lunch.  Glazed eyes
are fixed on the snail like speed of the
second hand as it inches toward that long
awaited moment.  Like runners in starting
blocks, raising slowly, powerfully, each student braces against the desk for that firmness
of start that will catapult them past opponents,
over the teacher and through the door to lunch,
glorious lunch.

Yet down the hall, students caught up
in the enthusiasm of a good topic or excellent
presentation perceive the clock as a spoiler.
A class has ended before its time.  A thought
will have to wait until tomorrow, unless a
brief audience with the teacher is possible
after class.

Both classes are affected by time.  There
is nothing inherently wrong with the hour by
hour concept of instruction.  It's easy to
schedule.  The problems begin when the teacher
has no imagination in the use of the time.
Let's think of fifty minutes in a "control
model" and then fifty minutes in a "learning
model".

In a control model, the clock is the
dictator and the teacher its willing servant.
"It's time to begin."  "Bored or not you'll
have to listen for ten more minutes."  "Stop
watching the clock."  "We have to cover this
material by the end of class."  The classes
look pretty much the same from start to finish.

All business.  No breaks.  Hold them till the
last second.

In the learning model, the teacher views
the fifty minutes as possessing an unlimited
number of combinations.  The first five minutes
might be "Calm down", "Get your breath", "Who
won the basketball game last night?"  "Who's
the boy that walked you to class?"  The next
five minutes might be directions.  "Here's
what we're going to be doing today.  It's
tough but I'll help you with it.  These are my
expectations."  The next twenty to thirty minutes might take this form:  Unit work or fifteen minutes each on two units.  The last five
minutes you might say "You worked well today".
"I thing we've accomplished something."
"Thank you for coming."  "Take a few minutes
to talk with a friend."  "What's for lunch?"

The fifty minute class period can be as
rigid as it looks on the class schedule, or
the fifty minutes can merely be the limits
within which any combination of time and events
can be structured.  Remember firm and fair?
How did this sound?  Firmness is having things
to do.  Fairness is accomplishing goals with
common sense planning.

## STUDENTS WON'T LISTEN TO ME
## BUT THEY'LL DO ANYTHING FOR MR. KERR

We all would secretly like to possess the charismatic leadership skill of a Knute Rockne. The problem is that different leadership styles are rarely as distinct in practice as they are in an education class. Here's how to sort them out.

Styles of leadership in a class might flow from task oriented through democratic to laissez-faire. There is no one style that is effective all the time. It's a matter of which style, when.

If you begin your class with objectives and goals that you have developed, then you will probably be more task oriented and direct. As the class proceeds, you may be doing less talking and the students will be participating more. Towards the end of the day it may be that you have no specific objectives so you decide to let the kids discuss anything they would like to.

Task oriented leadership behavior sounds like this: Today we're going to do this, this, this, and this. At 11:30 we'll have some discussion. At the end of class you'll have some time to yourself.

Democratic leadership behavior sounds like this: "Do any of you have any thoughts on why the United States enjoys a pivotal position in world politics?" You're setting the objectives but others are participating with their views.

Laissez-faire leadership behavior sounds like this: "Take five minutes to relax or

14

get ready for your next class". The students
have this time to themselves. It might be a
chance to talk, or perhaps ask you a question.
This private time might serve as a nice re-
ward for a job well done. You simply bow out
for a while.

# I DIDN'T UNDERSTAND ONE WORD IN THAT LECTURE

Nothing is more frustrating than to have somebody talk over your head. As a listener, you want to understand, but the vocabulary being used to explain a concept is too complex. The words simply have no meaning. They could have meaning, but sometimes it seems as though the talker really doesn't want you to understand. Surely he can see that nobody is understanding a word he is saying. Why is this done? Here are a couple of guesses.

A big vocabulary silences a lot of questions. Questions have a way of sounding dumb when not asked in the appropriate situational dialect. The novice who asks a question risks showing that he doesn't understand. A lot of classrooms work this way. Nobody asks a question because nobody wants to look stupid and nobody understands a thing that is being said but nobody wants to "look" stupid. Instead they sit and nod, occasionally smiling, hoping the teacher won't ask anyone to explain anything.

Adjusting your vocabulary to the understanding level of your students is the key to explaining anything. Any vocabulary level will function descriptively if it has meaning. You can accomplish this by giving a new word meaning in a context relevant to the listener and then proceeding with your explanation. Explaining clearly and slowly at the start of a lesson permits you to develop more complex concepts later in the lesson. Remember, fairness is helping students understand, not assuming that they do. If words have no meaning they won't be learned. Teacher questions like "Is this clear?" "Could I explain it differently?" "Should I slow down?" "Is this making any

sense?" These are all good ones to ask. The
trick is to ask them and mean what you say.

## I CAN TELL BY YOUR QUESTION
## YOU WERE'NT PAYING ATTENTION

In a room where a teacher lets it happen, each kid will need an answer to at least five questions. All your teacher training is reduced to one simple requirement -- stamina. If you welcome the interactions, kids will ask anything, anytime, anywhere. If you don't welcome them, you won't have to worry about getting tired. Kids won't ask you much at all. How you respond to questions will determine how many and what kind of questions you get asked.

If you are short, impolite, quick, resentful or impatient, only the bravest students will venture a question. Some teachers seem to resist too many questions because it slows them down. So the teacher behaves in such a way that no questions get asked except by the smartest of students. Consequently, no questions are heard from the kids who may really need clarification. Good for the teacher who doesn't want to answer questions, but too bad for the kids who are confused and afraid to ask.

If you welcome questions with genuineness, sincerity, interest, and patience, you won't believe the types and numbers of questions you'll get. You can encourage questions with this type of statement, "There are no dumb questions. The only dumb thing is to have a question and not ask it."

## WHAT IF SOMEBODY ASKS ME
## A QUESTION I CAN'T ANSWER?

Very early in the task of teaching, the
problem of how much knowledge is too much
knowledge arises. Does an elementary math
teacher need to have the math background of a
nuclear scientist? More times than not, a
teacher's obsession with being cognitively or
informationally slick will result in nobody'
learning anything. In the interest of lesson
plan flow, the teacher never once looks at
the students to see if they are comprehending
the lecture. The reason for this behavior is
simple. A question, particularly a divergent,
tangential question, might not have a pre-
pared-for answer. To not have the answer is
to lose respect. Right? Wrong!

Remember, you're a teacher. You don't
teach unless someone learns. The reason you
become comfortable with your subject matter
is so that what you discuss will be understood and learned, not so that you can appear
infallible or omnipotent.

If you set yourself up as the fountain
of perfection, somebody will challenge you
with questions you can't answer. Don't try
to be perfect and you won't look foolish if
you're not. If you don't know an answer or
aren't sure about something, admit it. Say
something like: "I don't know the answer now,
but rather than guess or mislead you, I'll
check it out later and let you know." Another
way is to say "I don't know but maybe somebody
here does. Does anybody know the answer?"

The big thing is to not try to deceive
anybody.  You're a teacher not a computer.
In the interest of intellectual honesty, why
not be honest.  You may feel a little unpre-
pared the first time you give a lecture but
it gets easier.  Most kids will appreciate
your fallibility.  Kids will see you as bright-
er for knowing what you don't know.

## MR. WELLER TOLD ANOTHER ONE
## OF HIS LOUSY JOKES TODAY

There is absolutely no substitute for
well planned humor in a classroom setting.
Don't take yourself so seriously that you
can't laugh at your own mistakes.  We've all
had teachers who never seemed to enjoy anything.  Whenever something awkward happened
to them, the kids could hardly hold back thé
laughter and rarely did.  It's one thing to
be laughed with and quite another to be
laughed at.  If you goof, you good.  Note it
with something like "That figures," or "Why
does this always happen to the coordinated
ones."

Beginning of class humor, middle of class
humor and end of class humor can be very
effective as lecture styles.  How about starting the class with a thought for the day?
Today's thought is "Don't dive in a pile of
leaves with a wet sucker."  It may set a good
tone for the class.  It sure beats yelling
"Shut up!" or "Class!"

Middle of the class humor has a way of
resurrecting interest.  A decent joke, even
a bad one, introduces some comic relief that
may keep students attending to you long after
they would quit with another teacher.  You
don't have to be funny.  Just wait and see
what happens.  If the joke dies, that has a
way of being funny, too, if you let it be.
A good class groan can be very therapeutic.

End of the class humor is perhaps the
best of all.  It follows the third law of
show business:  Always leave 'em laughing.

A good riddle, anecdote or story will send
kids away with a smile. It has a way of bring-
ing them back the next day with a smile. Kids
love puns. They also appreciate teachers who
care enough to try to make a classroom enjoy-
able.

## YOU'RE GOING TO LOVE
## WHAT WE'RE DOING TOMORROW

You're talking to the class and it's obvisous nothing is occuring. Heads are on desks or in chins. Eyecontack is in any direction except towards you. The closk becomes the preoccupation of thirty sets of eyeballs. Remember how you knew that the bell rang when the-second-hand-hit-the-two-after-the-big-hand-was-on-the-one. Several options are open to you in an instance of obvious boredom or fatigue.

It's easy to buy the bad seed argument under these trying circumstances. You just blame the kids with whatever teacher talk you are most familiar. "You're lazy." "You shouldn't be concerned about lunch at 11:30." "Friday is just like any other day of the week." "This has been a problem class all year." "I've heard about this class and your critics were right." "There is nothing wrong with this material. You're just not paying attention." Almost always these phrases are directed toward the entire class, which means they don't offend anybody, but they do arouse class indignation.

What does this type of talk produce? Nothing! If anything happens it's only in the direction of increased antagonism. The teacher retaliated. The agression serves them right. Kids look humble. It may get quiet. They may sit back in their chairs. But it's a cheap thrill and you'll pay for it the rest of the year.

You have another alternative, but you have to practice it. It may be uncomfortable at first, but that's because, even though we know it's not true, we want to believe that teachers don't really goof things up. But teachers do. How could thirty kids go sour simultaneously and exhibit the same boredom without it being something they all see. Maybe they all see the teacher.

By eighth period, most history teachers wish the civil war had ended in a draw. Math teachers wish Pythagoras hadn't been so curious. The chemistry teacher wishes for the simplicity of Hippocrates' four humors. The passing of a day has a way of making a topic that was interesting, funny and informative in the morning classes, a trial by fire during the afternoon.

You may have had an idea that "couldn't miss" until the class whiz kid asked you "the" question you couldn't answer. That great idea for Monday sounded good at home, but didn't work at school. Maybe you got so wrapped up in the idea you forgot about the kids. When they slow you down by not understanding, your feelings get hurt. It was a perfect lesson and they wrecked it. You act out against the students when the source of the difficulty was you or your delivery.

Just because an idea doesn't play well, it doesn't mean it's a bad idea. It may just need a different delivery. If an idea goes well in the first period classes, but not later, it may be that you've lost your enthusiasm for it and you're communicating that fact.

Some ideas are just plain junk.  If they
don't work, don't use them again.  But don't
stop trying.  Anyone that says a student doesn't
recognize when a teacher is trying his hardest
is probably the person who does the same lessons
over and over.  Kids will tell you how you're
doing with their faces and eyes.  Use the information.  How many times were you bored stiff,
saw everybody else was, and watched the teacher
face the board and keep on writing.  You may
not see the boredom when you face the board
but you can't see anybody smile either.

## ONLY TEN PLAYERS WILL DRESS FOR AWAY GAMES

There's nothing like a little competition to motivate. Right? Not always. Generally, competition for scarce resources, whether it's gasoline, grades or a spot on the roster, brings out the worst in everybody. What makes competition in the classroom even more devastating is that the kids have to come back into the competitive environment every day.

Self confidence is more important than any isolated fact. Facts can be a vehicle for enhancement of self confidence. If a fact threatens self confidence, perhaps the fact should be tempered in service of a greater fact; that a child should learn to believe they can learn.

Competition for grades or approval can polarize attitudes, isolate individuals (the losers) and totally destroy any good learning environment. For every one competitor we generate, we probably convince thirty kids that there is very little they can ever hope to compete for and win. Competition generates a false sense of omnipotence in the winner and a destructive sense of impotence in the loser. This kind of polarity will destroy a classroom and the children in it. You won't get a chance to teach because you'll be too busy being a referee. You didn't get certified to wear a striped shirt and blow a whistle. If you're going to have students competing, plan for enough resources that everyone can win.

## IF YOU DON'T DO THE MATH IN CLASS
## THEN YOU CAN DO IT AFTER SCHOOL

Pupil behaviors can be a source of valuable information. Classroom and individual communication breaks down when the teacher refuses to regard a pupil's behavior as a way of communicating. You have the option of either welcoming the behaviors as symptoms or being threatened by them. How you perceive them will dictate how you react to them.

A kid forgets his math book, doesn't pay attention, makes excuses and disrupts class. Does he hate you? Does he hate what you are doing? Or does he hate what you are making him painfully aware of in himself: the fact that he doesn't understand as easily as others. If you think he hates you, you'll probably do something bright like hate him back. You'll do what people do when they hate someone. You'll hurt him as quickly as you can with whatever will hurt the most. Maybe you'll ask him a question you know he can't answer. Usually, it's the subject matter that becomes the weapon. More math after school is the answer. Extra homework. Maybe an F for the six weeks grading period. These teacher behaviors rarely if ever work, except to punish and generate more hostility.

You're never going to make anybody like something by punishing them with it. Maybe what that math kid needed was less complex math or no math for a while. Certainly, he doesn't need more math as punishment for not liking math. Maybe he just needs to talk to somebody about why math is difficult. A positive attitude toward learning is much more important than the accomplishment of any isolated task.

27

# I DID EVERYTHING BUT TELL
## YOU WHAT TO STUDY

"What's going to be on the test?" "I can't tell you or it wouldn't be a test! Just study the chapter: seventy pages!" "A forty-five minute test on World War II seems fair enough. Doesn't it? Use both sides of the paper if necessary." Sound familiar?

Expectations during instruction should be clear and unambiguous. A student has a right to know what he or she is expected to learn. Why should a student waste energy trying to determine what to study, when the same amount of energy could be used to master a specific instructional objective. The student should not have to guess which list of ten words will be on the test. He should be told which list. Then he can devote his energies to learning the list he knows will be on the test. Remember the math tests you took that included problems you had never seen before? Wasn't it fun, educational and motivating to flunk? Trick questions rarely motivate. No classroom procedure is more unfair than testing over material that nobody knew would be on the test.

Some teachers test in compulsive secrecy and employ the severest of measures, grade curves and evaluation. Remember the motivation to excell when you were told that your class of thirty students would have two A's, four B's, eighteen C's, four D's and last but not least, two F's. This announcement can always be counted on as a motivator to the two students who received F's on last week's chapter test.

Other teachers are open and straight forward about what is expected and what will be evaluated. When your tests become more important than the kids you're teaching, your priorities need some reviewing. Firmness is instructional objectives and expectations. Fairness is letting students know specifically what needs to be learned and helping them achieve success.

## THE TEST TOMORROW IS VERY IMPORTANT.
## IF YOU HAVE ANY QUESTIONS

Most students think of studying as sitting at a desk, staring at a text and trying to remember at one hundred words a minute. They try to read twenty pages of American History like it was the great American novel. Other models of effective studying might include two kids quizzing each other, a written time line of events in the chapter, or reading a chapter with paper and pencil in hand to help reinforce dates, events, etc.

Telling them when to study might also be helpful. Explaining why cramming rarely works might be a good topic of discussion. Good studying might follow a sequential plan: (1) read to familiarize (2) read to remember (3) oral quiz to retain (4) write to recall, and (5) practice test for confidence. Suggestions like these might help some kids be rewarded with good grades for systematic studying.

Modeling is important during study period. Don't give students a study period and then go to the teacher's lounge. What you're modeling is an incredible lack of interest. Help them study. Show them how. Ask kids how they study. Maybe they can tip each other off on some learning tricks. Model that you are genuinely interested in their successes.

Firmness is telling them they have to study. Fairness is showing them how to study. Don't expect a student to be interested in someting you don't show any interest in.

## YOU HAD BETTER KEEP
## YOUR EYE ON THAT KID

As a student, did you ever hear "This is the worst group I have ever had". "You are an embarrassment to the school building."

What you hear about a class from other teachers, the grapevine, the principal, etc. may influence how you behave toward a class on first meeting and subsequently. Some helpful teacher will say, "This class needs control." After a few years the class, by reputation, becomes a mob. Every teacher heard the same information and responded with control. What the class may need is a breather from control or a different type of control. Expectations structure perceptions and perceptions have a way of structuring behaviors. If you behave like a warden, you should expect "prison dumb" students.

A single student may also travel under the label of someone to watch. Any student whose behavior is monitored very closely will eventually good up. Unfortunately for students with a reputation, teachers are quick to make sure "they" don't get away with anything. What is alright for one student to do is unacceptable for another student because it might lead to something else or get out of control.

The lesson here is to ignore school wide gossip about students. Try the very best that you can to form your own opinions. You may befriend a student others have not gotten along well with and have an influence on him.

## IT SEEMS LIKE HE YELLS ALL THE TIME

Be a nice person. Don't let them get
away with anything. Be helpful. Be too nice
and they'll take advantage. Don't smile until
Christmas. Confused? Try thinking in these
terms.

Certain types of pupil behavior will
disrupt any learning environment. If a student
decides to start yelling across the room, that
qualifies as a disruption. This is the time
to be direct, censuring and firm. You want
the disruption to stop, so do whatever it takes
to get it stopped; a private word outside, a
conference or a visit to the office. This is
a behavior problem. If you're going to confront, this is the time.

The context to be supportive, considering
and patient is when you are trying to facilitate
learning. Sending a student to the office or
yelling at him won't make him answer any better.
If everyone has failed a test, maybe some
dialogue is in order, but not intimidation.
Confrontation in learning contexts serves no
long term motive except resentment.

Be firm when you want something to stop
and supportive when you want something to start
or keep going. You want to stop a student
from being disruptive, but you want to encourage
him in his learning.

## WHO STARTED IT?
### HE STARTED IT. NO, HE STARTED IT.

Within the classroom, your reputation as
an arbitrator will be directly related to the
number of "correct calls" you make. Effective settlement of disputes often requires the
wisdom of Solomon. Correct calls are always
carefully calculated by students as well as by
each of the witnesses. Each witness knows
that sooner or later their number may come up
and your wisdom or lack of wisdom will touch
them.

The main consideration in any dispute is
"Do you know all the facts?" Kids are con-
scious of this soft underbelly of justice.
Hence, they will search for witnesses to help
reconstruct the crime in their favor. Always
this reconstruction is done at full volume,
with an opposition and his supporters chiming
in melodiously. Questioning the participants
doesn't help. Each has his own interpretation.
Each description is probably reasonably truth-
ful. If you look to the more trusted of the
two, screams of partiality will resound.

The best way to avoid having a small disruption turn into a tag team match is to not
ask the question "Who started it?" Both kids
start talking at precisely the same time.
This timing is usually incredible. The first
kid to explain always has the advantage and
the other kid knows it. Don't let the verbal
battle get started. Here's why.

You probably didn't see it get started.
You probably walked in the middle or near the
end. Why take a chance on blaming the wrong
person? Remember firm and fair. Try this
instead.

33

If you sense that you didn't see all the action, then arbitration will only get you in trouble. Chances are you don't really care who started it anyway. You probably just want it stopped. Why not say something like this. "I don't care who started it. I want it to stop and I don't want it to start again." Everybody escapes with their pride intact and you are in control again.

## BUT MR. HALE LET US DO THIS LAST YEAR

You've been through this a million times
in every year of public school.  Now is your
chance, to not let it happen in your room.

In any new room with new kids, the expectations and privileges from other years and
other teachers remain near the surface.  Your
expectations may be new to them.  What went
on last year may interfere with your explanations of what is expected this year.  It's
"fair" to give a warning to a student who is
having trouble with one or more of your expectations.

A warning says several things.  Firstly,
it tells the student that you can and will
monitor his behavior.  Secondly, and most im-
portantly, a warning eliminates the cry "You
didn't tell me.  How was I supposed to know?"
"Mrs. Smith didn't mind if we did that."  Unclear expectations are difficult to follow.
Allow for some initial confusion and interference from a student's prior experiences.
Thirdly, the warning provides an opportunity
for clarifying an expectation.  Now the responsibility for another error is off your
shoulders.  You can always say that you gave
an individual warning.  Anybody can goof once,
for any number of reasons.  Many reasons might
be legitimate.  But a goof after a clear, fair,
reasoned warning is more easily attributable
to the child.  Other students see the warning
as more fair than punishing an offender for
something they didn't know anything about.
We've all had teachers who seemed to build
traps for kids by presenting unclear expectations.  The unfortunate part is that it's
always the same child who zigs when he should
zag, gets yelled at, and eventually gets

trapped more than anybody else.  The difference
between fair and unfair is a warning.

## IT'S ALL IN USING THE
## RIGHT VOICE AT THE RIGHT TIME

In a tone as firm and terrifying as any
principal's admonition to be careful "or else",
Clint Eastwood turned towards a would be as-
sailant and whispered "If you don't put that
knife down, you won't believe what happens
next even while it's happening." He was very
effective. It was all in his tone of voice.
The fact that he is 6'4" and 200 lbs. had
nothing to do with it!

Experienced teachers learn very quickly
the manipulation of voice tone to achieve
certain desired behaviors. The voice tones
sound something like this:

An everyday, I'm-going-to-talk-about-
saturn voice tone is the one that should be
used most often. It's a procedural, positive,
regular voice tone. It's the tone you might
use to tell someone you were real proud of
what they had done today. Go ahead, try it out.
"Anyone here have to go to the restroom?" or
maybe, "Would someone go to Mr. Clark's room
and get the globe?" Let's call this voice one
(1).

Voice two will make more sense if I explain
voice three first. Voice three is a glass
breaking, ear shattering, you've lost your cool
voice. It's the voice of a late Friday afternoon in February, when you decide that enough
is enough. It may have immediate shock value
but the outcomes are short lived. Here's why.

You can not possibly outshout thirty kids
that want to "not hear you", especially high
school kids. Start shouting too much in Sep-
tember and by Christmas you'll be shouting all

37

the time. It will seem as if all thirty kids had gone deaf. Kids will be quieter when it's to their advantage to be quiet. Enter voice two.

Voice two is a firm voice. It's an informative tone that suggests it will be to a student's advantage to quiet down. You can get a lot done with this voice. It has a way of getting pupil attention without excitement. It's a calm, controlled, I-wouldn't-do-that-anymore-if-I-were-you voice. It's a come-over-here voice without the excitement. Principals use the number two voice very effectively. For that matter so do all the strong silent hero types. Have you ever heard John Wayne ask "What do you think, boys?" in falsetto?

# TWO IS COMPANY BUT THREE IS A CROWD

Nothing is more frightening to a new teacher than the thought of seeming not in control in front of an entire classroom. Likewise, students seem to know more keenly than any observer when a teacher has crossed over the line from legitimate authority to personal abuse. It's one thing to correct somebody for an error in judgement. It's quite another thing to humiliate someone in front of the entire class. Remember how good you felt and how much you liked the teacher after he just told the whole class what a dope you were? "I swear young man, I don't know how you passed the third grade".

Who the correcting is done in front of, and how much correcting takes place makes all the difference in class control. After enough abuse, even the class trouble-maker becomes a cult hero. The kids collectively react to the teacher with more hostility than the teacher can possibly handle. The respect of the class may be lost, and justifiably so, because your authority has been misused. Try this.

When someone is out of order, walk back to their desk and tell them you would like to see them privately. Outside the room, any corrective statements can be made, any agreement reached, without the student losing face. In private, a student will admit to making an error in judgement, that in public, he would refuse to admit to. A plan for behavior improvement can be worked out that is tailored to the individual student. All this without the interference of other students. Plus, your agreement with him doesn't have to be made to apply to anybody else. I can think of nothing more embarassing than being corrected in front of an entire class. Embarassment might generate immediate quiet, but rarely does it generate respect. A private talk, whether on the spot or after class, is always preferable to classroom confrontation. One on one, your appeal can be as individualized as your instruction.

## IF YOU DON'T QUIET DOWN
## YOU'RE GOING TO BE HERE AFTER SCHOOL

You may recall the warning of your college supervisor or the teacher with whom you student taught; "They'll test you, back up what you say you'll do." How do you back up a threat to throw somebody out of your class if you're 5'4", 120 lbs. and new. Remember the kid you're trying to threaten is 6'4", 200 lbs. and has not been having a good day. He also has nothing to lose. They'll just imprison him. Here are a couple of suggestions.

Don't let your new found legitimate authority cloud your judgement about what you can and can't actually pull off. Remember, if they all wanted to talk all day, you probably couldn't stop them. 6'4" is pretty big. Why make a verbal threat in the first place? A stare might do the trick. Moving toward the area of disruption might be next. See what a little silent authority can do first. Your next move might be an invitation for a private discussion in the hall or a very quiet "see me after class" in a number two voice tone.

If it gets down to an if-then statement, then an open-ended statement might be the solution. "If this keeps up, then it's going to go bad for you." Leave the consequences open ended. Let the student's imagination work its little wonder.

If-thens always have a threatening dimension to them. Threats have arousal qualities. Rarely do they function to shorten a disruption. They always invite a test. Some kids characteristically accept the invitation. Some kids rarely do. Explain what you expect

in a situation.  Explain why.  Warn once.
Don't dare anybody in front of a group.
Discipline privately.

## MR. BENDER ALWAYS COMES TO THE AWAY GAMES

Any vocation has two kinds of people in
it; people who are in it and people who are
involved in it. It's not very hard to tell
which person is which. People who enjoy what
they do, do more than they have to. People
who don't enjoy what they do, do as little
as possible.

Teachers can be described in the same
kinds of terms. Those who teach because
they happen to be teachers and those who teach
because they like to teach. Kids know the
difference. One way they find out is by the
teacher's level of involvement at school.

Low involvement looks like this. Teacher
arrives on time, goes to lounge, teaches classes,
eats in lounge, prepares in lounge, teaches
classes and goes home. Always doing what is
required and never more.

High involvement looks like this. The
teacher plays a little softball with kids before school, talks with kids before classes,
observes and interacts in extra-curricular
settings with kids, attends school-kid functions
like sporting events, music activities, parti-
cipates in dress-up days and bakesales, etc.
It's the extra little things that matter to
kids; a game of war ball, a yearbook sponsor-
ship, an outing that requires a chaperone. A
student will repay a hundred times over, a
moment of personal advice or encouragement pro-
vided by an interested teacher.

It seems only fair that a teacher should
show the kind of interest in kids that he or
she expects of students during classtime. Maybe you could go in to the bandroom and listen

43

to a rehearsal or watch the football team practice. Behaviors like these will tell the students a great deal about your interest in what they do.

## IF YOU'RE NOT HERE WHEN
## WE LEAVE, YOU'LL GET LEFT

What primer for new teachers would be
complete without some tips on field trips?
With little kids (K-4) the buddy system with
lots of parents, is the best organizational
plan. Provide for pre, during, and post
potty stops, occasional rest stops, easily man-
ipulated food and appropriate level, high
interest entertainment. The ballet will rarely
stimulate third graders. A farm with lots of
little animals to touch and feed would be an
outstanding field trip.

Junior high kids are ready for anything.
Museums, ball parks, sports activities, factory
field trips, vocational field trips, i.e.,
firehouses, are excellent. Strict grouping and
too much teacher organization will spoil a
junior high field trip. Trying to personally
shepherd thirty-five thirteen year olds will
just give you a giant excedrin headache. En-
forcing hand holding is inadvisable. Explaining the environment, describing responsibilities
and "suggesting" traveling in groups seems to
work pretty well. Don't hurry back to school.

Let the situation suggest the structure.
Try to have a good time yourself and suggest
a rendezvous time thirty minutes before you
return to school. Suggest a watch for each
group. Let some kids travel with you. The less
adventurous students will want to be with you
anyway.

High school kids will definitely want to
be left alone. They do not want any adventure
to look like a chaparoned adventure. Explain
your expectations. Let them be responsible
for their own actions. If somebody gets in

trouble, it does not reflect on you or your
school. It reflects on the kid. And tell
them so. If you think someone might not know
how to behave in a setting, explain your expectations before the trip and offer some
suggestions. If there is any doubt about a
student's ability to take care of himself,
take him with you.

## GUESS WHAT MR. RAY'S FIRST NAME IS

Remember how excited you got when you found out that your teacher's first name wasn't Mr. or Mrs.? You just wanted to run around yelling "Thelma"! "Her name's Thelma!" "Let's call her Thelma and see what she does." The problem is a familiar one. What do you do if a student starts calling you by your first name?

Try to assess motivation. It's either to bother you or because they like you. If they like you, try this. "It doesn't bother me if you use my first name, but other students might begin to call other teachers by their first names. Other kids would get in trouble, and it could cause problems for me." Basically, it's just a contextual explanation of role relationships.

If a student is baiting you, use whatever recourse you have at your disposal. You might try a private discussion, parents, or the principal. Above all, do not ignore it if it bothers you. Confront the student. Ask him to stop. Explain the consequences of not stopping.

Sometimes this statement works: "Call me whatever you are comfortable with." In schools, kids are most comfortable with what is natural. What is natural is usually Mr. or Ms. or Mrs. or Miss somebody. Shortened versions might appear like Mr. B or Mrs. C. Spoken in positive tones, these addresses can be indicative of very positive classroom environments. "Hey, stupid" is rarely a term of endearment.

47

## MR. BROOKS, YOU SOUND JUST LIKE
## MR. BENDER AND MR. WELLER

You're a new teacher and not as sure of yourself as you would like to be. You've read this little primer and you're still nervous. Here's one more hint to help you during the first few exhausting weeks of a new teaching job.

Ask a few students who the best teacher is in the building. You should be able to tell without asking, but it doesn't hurt to check. Once you find this out, try this little procedure. You might try to observe this teacher whom you've heard about, in settings outside the classroom. Watch this teacher during informal interactions with students. See when the teacher is available to the students. Watch how he or she treats the students. Even listen to his or her voice and manner.

Going a little farther, you might ask if you can sit in on a few lectures during your free period or maybe team teach a class or two. The association will be good for you and the modeling may be very effective. It's no shame to model yourself after the best. Find out or watch for the best and see it there is anything in their style that is compatible with the direction in which you wish to develop.

## A MONDAY MORNING IN TEACHING
## IS STILL A MONDAY MORNING

Sometimes teaching is just plain work.
You'll get up, go to your job, do what's
expected and come home. You'll work around
people you don't like, and work with people
you do like. You'll have highs and lows, good
days and bad. Some kids won't like you no
matter what you do. Other kids will always
like you, even if you're not particularly nice.

You'll be caught up in the practical day
to day functioning of the school. You'll
have to manage thirty kids in a confined space
for a prolonged period of time, in service of
a community mandate to teach. Parents will
question your teaching style, kids will cry for
relevancy, adversaries may try to confound your
boldest efforts to innovate. If you're good,
others may be jealous.

You will be adapting to an environment
very unlike the university classroom. An
environment where people are painfully honest.
You'll be asked to do things that seem to con-
tradict all that you've been made aware of in
college. How do you live with all the contra-
dictions?

Each day should be a new day. Each kid's
problem should be as important as any other's.
Strive for excellence through honesty. Encourage and stimulate to the best of your ability. Treat students as you would like to have
been treated and never stop getting excited by
the little things.

# INTRODUCTION

Part II is written for the public school teacher who has been asked to supervise a student teacher. The supervision process is complex. Relevant questions might include, "How will I determine what behaviors are important to observe?" "How should I observe the student teacher?" "When and how should I conference?" "How will I evaluate the student teacher?" Helpful solutions to these and other questions are offered in succeeding chapters.

Included in Part II are options which allow an appropriate approach to supervising a student teacher. It is extremely helpful for the student teacher to know precisely what being a "good teacher" comprises. For instance, rather than telling the student teacher to be flexible, tell him in what situations he needs to be flexible. Again, don't tell him to be a hard guy, tell him when to be a hard guy. Prescribe in contexts, not concepts.

Remember that teaching is a process. The best way to teach a process is to model the process. Allow the student teacher the advantage of observing selected teacher models. Structure what the student teacher is to observe. Include such daily routines as opening a class, closing a class, answering questions, giving a test, and disciplining a student. Focus these observations on the verbal and nonverbal behaviors that occur in the classroom contexts.

Part I spoke of being firm and fair. Part II further considers firm and fair as an instructional goal. One will achieve fairness in his supervision if he follows some simple guidelines. Discuss objectives and expectations

on the very first day. Model and explain the
processes for achieving the stated objectives.
Evaluate on the objectives which have been
discussed and modeled. The supervisor sets
the tone for professional dialogue. This
professional dialogue then provides an atmo-
sphere for professional growth and development.

# CRITERIA FOR STUDENT TEACHER ASSESSMENT

The criteria for student teacher evaluation can be organized into four categories of characteristics. Each category has merit although each category differs in its utility effectiveness and ease of implementation.

## Intuitive/Folklore

The first approach is the intuitive/folklore approach. In this instance the supervisor evaluates the student teacher with the same criteria which the supervisor was evaluated when he performed student teaching. Likewise, criteria that seem appropriate for success in a particular building are often used. Consequently, a very unique set of criteria emerges which may be functional within a particular building but which may not reflect the type of criteria that relate to instructional effectiveness.

For example, some student teacher supervisors insist that classroom silence is a major behavioral objective. From a research point of view, the ability to sustain silence hardly holds up as a criteria for evaluation, although admittedly there are times when any student teacher should be able to enlist quiet in order to accomplish a task.

## Competency/Performance

Another popular set of criteria are professional competencies or observable behavioral acts which are thought to relate to teacher effectiveness. University professors are required to demonstrate how the objectives of their courses should materialize into an observable student teacher behavior. The problem with this approach to evaluation is that what emerges is an unmanageable list of competencies. The school supervisor neither understands the criteria nor wishes to impose them on the student teacher. The university supervisor has neither the time nor the patience to actively observe the student teacher exhibiting these competencies. Consequently, what happens is that the competencies exist, but traditionally, the model or approach that ultimately emerges is the intuitive/folklore approach.

## Pupil Gains/Achievements

The third type of criteria available for the evaluation of student teachers is pupil gains in achievement or attitude. While this is an admirable type of criteria, it requires that the student teacher demonstrate with pretest and post test scores that the pupil has actually profited from the instruction. This type of student teacher evaluation is time consuming, difficult to administrate and rarely practiced or understood by supervising teachers. Consequently, an observation like "They seem to really be learning with this student teacher" is about as close as we get to a pupil gains type of evaluation.

## Teacher Characteristics and Instructional Variables

The fourth type of criteria available for the evaluation of student teachers can be categorized into two separate systems. The first system can be called teacher characteristics.

These criteria relate to the personality, intellectual and interpersonal characteristics of the student teacher. A list of fifteen of these teacher characteristics is included in order that student teacher supervisors might begin to share a common vocabulary with university supervisors. This fourth set of criteria may be the most reasonable combination of the four systems. These criteria are recognizable to the supervisor, easily observed, and can be reliably recorded and managed.

## Cognitive and Intellectual Dimensions

### Broad interests

The student teacher should be willing to discuss topics other than school work with their students, either before class, after class, or during class discussions.

### Subject area prepared

The student should be able to systematically organize his subject matter for instruction, coordinate materials as well as know what they are talking about.

### Ability to explain

The student teacher, in response to a pupil question, should be able to provide several different levels of explanation. They should be able to reverse from a complex explanation to a simpler interpretation when necessary. A student teacher should make every effort to explain a complex idea in simple terms.

## Use of advanced organizers

The student teacher should begin a class
by stating the instructional objectives for
the class.  This list should reflect what will
be learned during the class as well as how the
class objectives organize into the unit objectives.

## Recognize individual differences

The student teacher should provide for
the scholastic, social, and physical strengths
and weaknesses of individual students through
curricular instructional or methodological
innovations.

## Personality Dimensions

### Consistent and predictable

The student teacher should be stable in
his behavior towards individuals during instruction.  The student should have a sense
of knowing what will happen next as well as
what is expected of him in the area of responsibility.

### Friendliness

The student teacher should relate to
pupils and peers in a manner which increases
the likelihood of continued interaction.
Typically, the friendly teacher gives more of
his personal time to the needs of individual
pupils.

### Nonpunitive

As a matter of style the student teacher
should be considerate and supportive.  Student

teachers define and enforce expectations but
should not be arbitrary and vindictive in doing
so.

## Organized and systematic

The student teacher should be deliberate
and considerate of the student's need for clarity.
the ability to attend to detail is an example
of this characteristic.

## Imaginative

The student teacher should be divergent
and curious during presentations. Presentations
and planning should tend to reflect and experi-
mental and personalized style.

## Recognize and admit mistakes

The student teacher should show a willingness to admit to not knowing a particular answer. If a mistake is made in judgment, the
student teacher should be willing to account for
that mistake to the pupils and supervisors.

### Perceptions of Self and Others

## Value the feelings of students

When students express concerns of mis-
givings about insturctional tasks, the student
teacher should be willing to listen and modify
the task if necessary.

## Exhibit self-confidence

While almost all student teachers are
nervous at the start of student teaching, it is
expected that with experience a degree of self-
confidence will emerge. This self-confidence

should be reflected in the ability to "think on one's feet" and not be disturbed with extraordinary classroom episodes such as discipline.

## Get along well in social contexts

The student teacher should demonstrate an ability to be personally effective in social situations other than the classroom. Participation in extracurricular activities, social gatherings, faculty meetings, etc., come forth as additional important contexts.

## Seem to enjoy teaching

The student teacher should "get into it" with extra time commitments, a willingness to go the extra mile for success, a desire to perfect and amplify instruction, and a generally positive approach to the task of instruction.

## Instructional Variables

A second system of evaluation criteria focus on the actual process of instruction. This list of nine variables have been shown to relate to pupil gain scores in attitude and achievement. These criteria should be employed during any episode of direct observation of student teacher instruction.

## Clarity

This variable takes the form of a beginning explanation of instructional objectives. The student teacher should provide explanations when questions are asked as well as demonstrate the ability to reduce complex ideas to simple explanations. The student teacher may use overheads, tape recorders, movies, or anything in order to achieve greater clarity. The willingness to review is an excellent example of this variable in action.

## Provides opportunity to learn materials during instruction

This variable is reflected in the student teacher's willingness to provide work sheets, to provide for active review and to provide the opportunity to ask questions. The supervisor should observe an active style of instruction that helps pupils master material during class.

## Enthusiasm

This variable takes the form of overt enjoyment of the instructional process, the use of humor, a smoothness or "with-it-ness" in the classroom. Likewise, the student teacher should show a willingness not to be distracted by "little things" at the expense of instructional effectiveness. This variable is generally reflected in overt enjoyment of the instructional act.

## Task orientation

Task orientation is accomplishing goals during instruction. At the end of class, the student teacher should have accomplished those goals that they intended and have made plans for the evaluation of the instruction.

## Provides for learning opportunities other than listening

The student teacher should provide for peer group activities, small group activities, opportunities for questions, field trips, movies, listening to tapes, and other activities that assist retention of instructional goals.

## Ability to explain at the appropriate level

The student teacher should demonstrate an ability to take a complex idea and reduce it to simple terms. The use of visuals will assist explanations. The use of a chalk board will also help. Verbal imagery and concrete examples might be of assistance. What the supervisor should observe is that the student teacher regards a lack of pupil understanding as something that he can correct through berter explication, rather than faulting an individual pupil.

## The use of student ideas during instruction

The student teacher might use student input before class, during class and after class. The student teacher should recognize pupil questions and inquiries during instruction and respect pupil contribution. The students should want to increase their participation.

## Supportive and non-critical during instruction

This variable relates to student teacher evaluation of pupil remarks. The student teacher should be facilitating and supportive of pupil observations and not be critical or non-supportive. Discipline problems may arise because the pupils have stopped interacting with the student teacher.

## Types of questioning

What the supervisor should observe is movement along a continuum from relatively simple, concrete types of questions to more abstract, complex, intriguing, divergent types of questions. The latter type of question tends to be regarded as the more positive instructional act.

While this list of fifteen teacher characteristics and nine instructional variables may not be all inclusive, these variables do form a systematic set of organizers that can be discussed in an initial conference with a student teacher and elaborated and commented upon in the formative evaluation. They may become a dimension of the final evaluation at the conclusion of the student teacher experience. Each one of these variables can be discussed with the student teacher in advance and progress along these variables cannot help but assist the student teacher in mastering the teaching act.

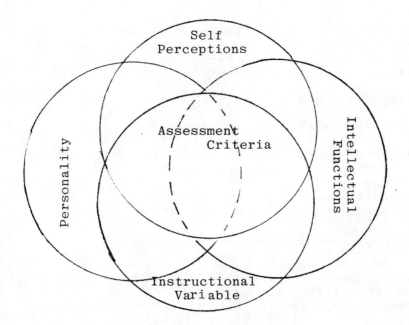

# THE PROFESSIONAL VOCABULARY

Following the identification of a supervisor criteria, it is possible for participants to communicate more specifically about the behaviors of the student teacher. The following questions should aid in the observation and subsequent counseling of the student teacher.

Each of the following nine categories has been subdivided into before, during, and after instructional contexts. This subdivision should assist the supervisor in diagnosing the particular area of ineffectiveness. Each subdivision includes questions that may be asked by the supervisor and a corresponding recommendation. The intent of this material is to encourage a professional, diagnostic vocabulary.

## Enthusiam

Before Instruction
1. Are you prepared with objectives?/ Know what you're going to do.
2. Have you rehearsed the content?/Review main points before class.
3. Have you included any motivational discussion before you start your lecture?/Make it interesting.
4. Do you plan any warm-up?/Tell a joke, riddle, ask about school athletics, music, boyfriends, etc.

During Instruction

1. Are you including any humor in your lesson?/Build some in.

2. Does your topic flow from one point to the next?/Know your stuff.
3. Are you enthused about the topic?/ Find something interesting in the material. Try to psych yourself up.
4. Are you varying your pace and style?/ Try induction or deduction.
5. Do you enjoy your own style?/Observe teachers with a style you like.
6. Are you allowing for spontaneity?/ Invite questions. Allow for student humor.

After Instruction

1. Are you satisfied with your presentation?/Change something. Alter topic. Involve students.

## Clarity

Before Instruction

1. Is the level of material appropriate?/ Use simpler terms in discussion. Move from simple to complex examples.
2. Are you planning for the student's abilities or interests?/Relate topic to their experiences.
3. Are you setting instruction goals?/ Use a simple, direct lesson plan.

During Instruction

1. Are you using advanced organizers?/ Tell the students what you hope to accomplish in your lesson, week, unit, etc.
2. Are you lecturing at the appropriate pace?/Slow down or recap when faces look confused.

3. Are you wandering or "free associating" during your lecture?/Put an outline on the board or prepare a handout.
4. Are you summarizing the main points of your lecture at the end of the class?/ Summarize instructional objectives.

After Instruction

1. Are you improving your lecture or lesson for the next time?/Throw out or change the parts that didn't work.
2. Would any type of media improve clarity?/ See about a film, tape, slides, overheads, etc.
3. Could the students offer any suggestions or participate more?/Ask them.

## Learning Opportunities Other Than Listening

Before Instruction

1. Are you using your free time or informal class time for instruction?/ Talk informally before class, before school, etc.
2. Are you planning for student involvement?/Make lesson plans which provide for student involvement.

During Instruction

1. Are students being forced to just listen?/Try learning centers, individualizing, projects, discussion, etc.

After Instruction

1. Are you available after class?/Don't always leave on the heels of the students.

2. Are you adjusting lesson plans to increase student involvement?/Renovate
   your plans. Add a new twist.

## Explanation

Before Instruction

1. Do today's lesson plans include opportunities for question from yesterday?/
   Do this as a matter of style.
2. Are you summarizing yesterday's objectives before you start something new?/
   It should be a standard procedure.

During Instruction

1. Are you responding to obvious or subtle
   confusion?/Watch faces and eyes. Respond to questions. Slow down.
2. Would media help?/Use it.
3. Are you being patient when kids have
   questions?/Give everyone a chance to
   ask a question. Don't hurry students
   who don't have immediate understanding.

After Instruction

1. Do students understand what you've
   covered?/Summarize important points .
   at the conclusion of class.
2. Are you allowing for discussion at the
   end of class?/Build it into your class
   time.

## Task Orientation

Before Instruction

1. Are your lessons well planned?/Know
   what you're going to do.

2. Are you organized?/Make sure you have everything you need.
3. Are you being goal oriented?/Have objectives.

During Instruction

1. Are you limiting digression?/Put objectives on the board.
2. Do you run out of time?/Assign minutes to objectives.

After Instruction

1. Record where you stopped./Adjust objectives to available time.

## Multiple Levels of Discourse

Before Instruction

1. Are you assuming too much vocabulary knowledge?/Explain complex terms with simple terms.

During Instruction

1. Are you confusing students?/Slow down and temper that college vocabulary.

After Instruction

1. Are kids asking for clarification?/ Take time with them. Explain in their vocabulary.

## Use of Probing Questions

Before Instruction

1. Are you building into your planning opportunities for divergent questiong?/ Make this an instructional objective.

During Instruction

     1. Create a climate for divergency./Model divergent responding.
     2. Pursue responses with more questions./ Listen keenly to responses.

After Instruction

     1. Respond to probing question in non-classroom contexts.

## Use of Student Ideas

Before Instruction

     1. Plan a warm-up topic of discussion then flow into lecture discussion.

During Instruction

     1. Are kids reluctant to participate?/Do they lack practice in discussion? Have they been discouraged from participating in other classes?
     2. Are they responding negatively to you during discussion?/Be non-judgmental of divergent responses.
     3. Are you reinforcing participation?/ Are your nonverbal cues positive?

After Instruction

     1. Do students' ideas really change your method?/If so, prove it.

## Negative Criticism

Before Instruction

     1. Are you assuming the worst from students even before you interact with them?/ Don't let predispositions influence you.

2. Are you throwing your weight and authority around?/Be less judgmental concerning nonacademic matters.

## During Instruction

1. Are you taking pupil reactions personally?/Solve problems as if you were a disinterested third party.

2. Is your discipline of behavior effecting your encouragement of ideas?/Behavior and ideas are independent.

3. Are you overacting to some behaviors?/Be firm about what is important. Don't sweat the little things.

## After Instruction

1. Are you holding a grudge?/Exhibit a short memory.

# ESTABLISHING CONFERENCING PROCEDURES

## The Initial Conference

The initial conference should take place before the first day of student teaching. The student teacher should not be "dropped off" at the door. The university supervisor should not be introduced to the public school supervisor four or five weeks into the student teaching experience. An initial meeting is a "must" not only for the university supervisor and the classroom teacher, but for the student teacher as well.

## Setting

An important dimension of the initial meeting is the setting of that meeting. It should be a private setting -- a private office or a conference room make excellent settings. It is inadvisable to visit the classroom and stand behind the teacher's desk during instruction and try to communicate criteria for evaluation. This often invites problems in retention, understanding and communication. The opportunity to answer questions will also be limited. A student teacher should understand that the initial conference is an important meeting. It is this meeting which sets the tone and organizes the whole student teaching experience.

## Goal Analysis

The initial conference provides an opportunity for the identification and sequencing of major objectives which the student teacher should master. An achievement continuum can be organized which highlights skills and projected dates of mastery of such objectives.

The process by which this achievement continuum is established is, again, a collective process between the university supervisor, school supervisor, and the student teacher. The student teacher should be made aware of the expectations of the school supervisor and the university supervisor. The student teacher should know what he has to do to achieve mastery and the projected date for that mastery. The continuum is a time line.

An initial assessment of the student teacher's strengths and weaknesses can be made in specific areas. For example, student teachers should have an opportunity to observe that they are characteristically strong in the areas of humor or enthusiasm, but not particularly strong in the areas of lesson planning or individualized instruction. This self disclosure permits the university supervisor and the school supervisor to incorporate planning and individualizing experience into the student teaching experience.

An interpretation of the final evaluation document is always helpful. Most university have such a document. Many times the student teacher rarely sees the document until the end of student teaching, and occasionally he does not see it then. If enthusiasm is one of the categories to be evaluated, the student teacher should be given data regarding the types of behavior which demonstrate enthusiasm. To keep this criteria a secret, or to explain ambiguously, is an invitation to problems.

## Formative Conferences

At about four weeks, it is helpful to have a conference where the university supervisor, the building supervisor, and the student teacher discuss the progress of the student teacher along the skill development achieving continuum. At about ten or eleven weeks it is helpful to have a formative evaluation. At this meeting, the evaluation form is actually filled in by the school supervisor, and that document is discussed.

The supervisor may solicit pupil observations of the student teacher along predetermined criteria and use these pupil reports as a major organizer for the formative conference. Pupils might be asked to fill out a form on the teacher's personal characteristics and on the teacher's instructional ability. This information may be very useful. Student teachers are often receptive to pupil feedback concerning their instruction. A personality conflict may have developed between the university supervisor and the student teacher, or between the school supervisor and the student teacher, which is a threat to the objectivity of direct observation.

The supervising teacher may want to ask the students specific questions that can be answered with more explanation. Two questions that help to diagnose particular strengths and weaknesses are:

1.  "If you could tell the student teacher one thing that you particularly like about his teaching, what would it be?"

2.  "If you could suggest one area of instruction where the student teacher might improve, what would it be?"

The answers to these questions may provide valuable insight into the pupils' perceptions of the student teacher's instructional strengths and weaknesses. The pupil evaluation data appear to be very powerful and provide an excellent opportunity to discuss achievement and mastery.

The non-productive formative conference is most likely to occur when the initial conference does not include goal setting, the establishment of a time line for goal achievement, or a discussion of the evaluative procedure. If an initial goal-setting conference does not occur, the student is left to decide what is important. His goals may be divergent with the expectations and goals of the university supervisor and the school supervisor. Confusion continues when a time table for the achievement of these goals is not determined in advance. Some goals may go unmet while other goals are mastered very early but are never recognized or evaluated. Finally, when the decision-making process or the evaluation process is not discussed, the student teacher has little knowledge of the procedure for evaluation. Consequently, any meeting or conference is going to come as a surprise and is not going to be productive.

## Summative Conferences

The summative conference should be the capstone event in student teaching experiences. The student teacher should be aware of the final evaluation of the university supervisor and the public school supervisor. Procedures for certification should be explained. Requests for recommendations should be voiced. If a grade is to be assigned to the student teacher, it should be decided on and discussed. No questions should be left unanswer-

ed. The continued contact with the supervisors should be assured to the student teacher.

In summary, conferences between the student teacher, the university supervisor, and
the school supervisor can be of two types.
They can be productive conferences where the
student teacher is accurately evaluated and
recommendations are made for improvement. Or
conferences can be non-productive. In a non-
productive conference an air of mystery sur-
rounds the conferencing process. None of the
participants know exactly what is going to
be said or in what context things are going
to be said. The conference can be reduced
to inuendo and prejudice. The personal
biases of the participants may surface and,
in general, the communication at the conference will be non-productive and non-prescrip-
tive. Nothing concrete is discussed, and
rarely, if ever, are concrete evaluations or
recommendations made.

### Guidelines for Successful Conferencing

1.  Have a three way initial conference be-
    fore the start of student teaching.
2.  Determine and explain criteria for eval-
    uation.
3.  Determine a timeline for goal attainment.
4.  Use a professional vocabulary during con-
    ferencing.
5.  Be diagnostic and prescriptive.
6.  Schedule conferences to allow time for
    discussion.
7.  Permit input from all sources.
8.  Always include all participants.
9.  Have an agenda at each conference.
10. Make every attempt to conclude the con-
    ference on a positive note.

11. Always have a formal summative confer-
    ence.
12. Avoid "war stories" or outdated anec-
    dotes.
13. Empathize with the possible anxiety
    of the student teacher.
14. Don't always sound as if you are telling
    or directing.  Ask questions.
15. Be open minded to additional information.

If a thousand student teachers were questioned on the most threatening or anxiety provoking event in their student teaching experiences, that event would probably be the visitation of the university supervisor to their classroom for a formal evaluation. A close second in producing high anxiety would be the visitation of the public school supervisor to their class for the purpose of evaluation. This type of anxiety is avoidable. A method for reducing this anxiety resides in the strategy of observation and the establishment of an environment in which observation becomes a facilitating process.

## Establishing an Observational Environment

The first step toward establishing a healthy observational environment is the development of trust between the public school supervisor and the student teacher. This trust is established through a common evaluative vocabulary and a clarity of goals. The conferencing procedure mentioned in the second chapter helps to establish this trust. Both the supervisor and the student teacher are aware that the student teacher is being evaluated along specific criteria, that the criteria will not change, and that direct observation of the student teacher is all a part of the evaluation process. The observation is not an end in itself. But, rather, it is a formative event designed to help the student teacher progress toward mastery of the criteria that will be used in a final evaluation.

The public school supervisor and the university supervisor should take the primary

responsibility in establishing this environment. They should clarify any misconceptions
that the student teacher has about the observation process. They should define the
evaluation criteria and explain that observation of the student teacher is designed to
help the student teacher. This initial trust
should continue as long as the supervisors are
diagnostic and prescriptive in their observation of the student teacher. The key to continued trust is observation of stated criteria, not the idiosyncratic observation of
unrelated events.

## When to Observe

A helpful way to sustain a trusting observational environment is to recognize that
the public school supervisor will be observing the student teacher all the time. How-
ever, these observations can be sub-divided
into informal non-instructive observations
and formal instructional observations. Examples of informal non-instructional contexts
include before class behavior with students,
after class behavior with students, the use
of free time as well as the use of the planning period. The informal observations might
also include the student teacher's interactions with other student teachers, with
students outside of their direct charge, and
with other colleagues. These informal moments
may be critical to the success of the student
teacher during instruction and to their ma-
triculation into the total school environment.
The attention of the supervising teacher to
these non-instructional moments and informal
contexts should provide the supervising
teacher with a perspective of the student
teacher's school-wide behaviors.

The formal evaluation process which
usually involves sitting in the classroom

should be introduced in a nonthreatening
manner. Announcing to a student teacher that
you are observing to make sure they are meeting a criterion increases the likelihood that
one will see what he wishes to see. It does
not insure that the behavior will occur in
one's absence.

An interesting idea for direct observation is a team teaching experience. An experience like this early in the semester will
allow the supervising teacher and student
teacher to work together, learn from each
other, and reduce the anxiety of having the
supervisor present in the classroom. As the
confidence of the student teacher increases,
the supervisor can participate less in the
class. Throwing the student teacher the keys
to the room and only appearing for formal
observations will only add to the anxiety of
the student teacher during instruction as
well as result in a distorted performance.
The supervising teacher is likely to see it
as a contrived performance on the part of the
student teacher. It may or may not reflect
the actual day-to-day classroom behaviors of
the student teacher.

In short, the methodology of informality
requires that the student teacher supervisor
observe the teacher in non-instructional
moments, and the methodology of direct observation at the formal level requires the student teacher supervisor to be non-threatening,
purposeful, and immediate in his provision for
feedback to the student teacher.

Several techniques are available for
recording and reporting the results of informal and formal observations. A very useful technique for recording informal observations is the anecdotal record. On a five
by seven card the context in which the student

teacher is observed can be recorded.  The
time and setting of the observation is recorded and the general impressions of the supervising teacher are recorded.  An excellent
strategy to record formal, direct observation
is with the use of rating scales.  Each observation is regarded as an independent event.
The criteria remain the same.  The student
teacher supervisor makes a formal observation
and then fills out an observation form.  Such
a form must list teacher instructional variables similar to those mentioned in chapter
two.  It is helpful not to rate the student
teacher while one is observing.  Above all,
keep accurate records of the observations
for use during any formative or final evaluations.

The formal evaluation process should be
immediately followed by a conference to
discuss the performance of the student teacher.  A prolonged period between observation
and reporting feedback increases anxiety and
makes the procedure of direct observation
suspect.  Again, it is the responsibility of
the classroom supervisor to establish the
type of environment within which both formal
and informal evaluations of the student
teacher can be discussed.

### Barriers to Effective Observation

Major threats to objectivity during
direct observation of student teachers include
selective exposure and frozen evaluation.
To even the most careful of student teacher
supervisors, these threats to objectivity
can damage the observational environment
and result in student teacher anxiety and
mistrust.

## Selective Exposure

A questionable evaluation is made on the
student teacher because the supervising
teacher or university supervisor has observed
the student teacher in a restricted or selective number of settings. Consequently, the
student teacher feels the supervisor is not
getting the "total picture". For example,
the supervising teacher may observe the
student teacher in settings where the student teacher is particularly uncomfortable
and not observe in those settings where the
teacher is unusually confident.

Solution: To avoid this observational
error, observe the student teacher in as
many settings as possible. Begin before
school by observing in the teacher's lounge,
through all the classes, lunch period, free
time, as well as interpersonal relationships
with colleagues. Selective exposure is perhaps the most critical error in terms of
evaluation of a student teacher. The more
observations one makes over divergent contexts,
the more effective the final evaluation will
be.

## Frozen Evaluation

One of the most unfortunate barriers to
effective observation is frozen evaluation.
Frozen evaluation occurs when a student teacher supervisor decides that the student teacher
isn't going to improve in a particular area
or similarly that the student teacher is doing
so well in an area that the supervisor need
not make any further observations. In either
case, the problem is that the student teacher
either is not being reinforced on the instructional variables which they have mastered, or
they are not being corrected on those

instructional variables that are inappropriate. When frozen evaluation occurs, the productivity and the environment for continued observation and trust diminishes. This may be the start of what often is called a personality conflict. The important thing to remember is to evaluate the student teacher with the criteria that were determined in the initial conference, to reinforce positively those things that are being performed well and to discourage or to provide alternative behavior patterns for those things that aren't being done correctly.

Frozen evaluation can be caused by three errors in the direct observation which reside within the personality make-up of the supervisor.

## Generosity Error

A possible cause of frozen evaluation is generosity error. This type of error results from a reluctance on the part of the supervisor to diagnose, prescribe, or evaluate the student teacher. As a matter of style, the supervising teacher is overly generous in his positive regard for the student teacher and much that could be improved upon goes unnoticed or goes uncorrected. Consequently, the student teacher does not get a full range of experiences or a full sense of the progress. An example of this is the student teacher supervisor who would say, "Oh, my student teacher is doing just fine, wonderful, no problems". This evaluation does not communicate very much in terms of how the student teacher is progressing along the different criteria. The student teacher may, in fact, be having serious problems in one or two of the areas. When the public school supervisor is too generous, a situation arises

where the student teacher does not attain
mastery on evaluation criteria and pays the
penalty of a bad evaluation by the university
supervisor.

## Solution

The supervisors should evaluate the
student teacher by making use of all available criteria.

## Severity Error

In the case of severity error, the student teacher supervisor has chosen to dis-
regard positive achievements by the student
teacher and is overly severe in his evaluation of the student teacher. This severity
within specific criteria begins to general-
ize to other criteria which are being accep-
tably performed and the result is a frozen
negative evaluation of the student teacher.

## Logical Error

In this type of observation error, the
student teacher supervisor assumes a certain
logical premise and based upon that premise,
makes an evaluation. For example, "that all
students should be in their seats at all times
is a cornerstone of good teaching". If the
student teacher supervisor subscribes to this
premise, and incorporates it into a decision
on evaluation, the process looks something
like this. The student teacher does not have
everyone in their seats, therefore, they are
not exhibiting good instruction. The first
premise may be inaccurate, but since it is
included in the evaluation reasoning, it generates a negative evaluation which may not
be accurate.

Solution:  Each of these sources of
error can be checked when they are recognized
as potential threats to observational objectivity.  The best way to hold them in check
is to constantly evaluate using the specific
criteria designated as critical to excellence
in student teaching.  Observe often.  Check
out your perceptions with other members of
the school staff.  Talk with students about
their perceptions of the student teacher.
Above all, do not assume a teacher is all
good or all bad.  But rather, assume that
they exel in certain criteria but are faulty
in others.  In this way the supervisor is
in a better position to produce an accomplished
multi-talented journeyman instructor.

In summary, the process of direct observation of student teachers should be explained
clearly and openly at the initiating conference with the student teacher.  The criteria
for observation, the formal, and the informal
dimensions of the observation should be explained.  The process of direct observation
should be regarded as an innate part of the
procedure.  Opportunities should exist through
direct observation for both the student teacher and the supervisor to move toward the
achievement of goals that have been set in the
initial conference.

## TEN MAJOR RECURRENT PROBLEM
## AREAS WITH STUDENT TEACHERS

Different student teachers are often
destined to make the same mistakes. For
example, it seems that every semester a student teacher arrives with a college vocabulary
on his sleeve. The instructional problems
caused by this disposition can be extensive,
and unless checked, will produce even more
problems as the semester progresses. The
ten major recurring problem areas will be
identified and potential time-tested solutions
will be offered.

### The Semantic Stratosphere

The student teacher often enters the
public school environment armed with his
collegiate vocabulary. He has learned to
discuss and think in lengthy terms, and has
been conditioned by university training to
use words that are particularly descriptive
but not necessarily a part of the public
school students' vocabulary. The student
teacher occasionally fails to make the transi-
tion from "university type" dialogue to
"public school type" dialogue. The latter is
that which is best understood by the public
school student. While a well-developed
vocabulary is commendable, a well-informed
student teacher should use words that are
clear and meaningful to the students whom he
is teaching. If not, the students become
frustrated and problems ensue. Students
may desire to be attentive and to listen, but
do not understand the terms being used by the
student teacher and thus, they begin to com-
plain about the teacher not explaining well.
Discipline problems can emerge from this as
students become more and more frustrated with
the inability to comprehend what is being
taught by the student teacher.

Solution: Caution the student teacher
against the use of words that may not be
understood by the pupils and encourage them
to explain new words extensively. When they
introduce a new word, they should take time
to provide synonyms or explanations that are
consistent with the vocabulary of the pupils
so that the students will begin to understand
the relationship between words they know and
the words that the student teacher is using.
When the new words are explained, they may
become part of the pupils' vocabulary. Student teachers use big words because they are
nervous. As they become more confident, the
use of the larger words will diminish.

## Can't Get Out of the Blocks

Student teachers often fail to recognize
the importance of an organized, deliberate
class "opening" procedure. Opening means
getting students organized and moving in the
direction of productive classroom activities.
Very often the student teacher simply does
not know what constitutes an opening procedure.
Often this procedure is not clearly pointed
out to the student teacher by the supervising
teacher. As a consequence, the student
teacher has trouble getting the classroom organized and getting the students to work.
The failure to open instructions effectively
creates a "ripple effect" in classroom management problems. The longer the class does not
know what to do, the more divergent each
student's behavior will become. For example,
a student teacher that goes into class and
begins to ask divergent questions like "What
do you want to do today?" is going to have
more of a problem getting the classroom started than the student teacher who goes in and
says, "This is what we are going to do today."

Solution: The public school supervisor
might model a successful opening procedure
or let the student teacher observe another
teacher who is effective in opening instruction.

## The Great American Lecture

A third problem area is the overuse of
the lecture method of instruction by the
student teachers. Student teachers use the
lecture method as a method of anxiety re-
duction. The lecture method is a high control instructional method that allows the
student teacher to be dominant and direct in
the classroom. It is not all wrong for the
student teacher to be using the lecture method
early in their experience, but after about
four weeks, or whenever the student teacher
feels he has control over the classroom,
the student teacher should begin to introduce some variability into their instructional
style. The reliance on the lecture method
also is a sign that the student teacher may
not be actively pursuing the mastery of other
instructional styles.

Solution: Demonstrate alternative instructional formats such as small group work,
learning centers, individualized packets, etc.
Suggest that the student teacher mix up and
alternate instructional styles.

## My Job Is to Evaluate and I'm Going To

The fourth problem area in supervision
is the student teacher who is excessively
judgmental and evaluative. Student teachers
very often forget that pupil discipline problems and management problems are something
quite different from a student's intellectual
behavior or social curiosity. The student

teacher needs to be evaluative and judgmental
regarding pupils' classroom behavior, but
this should not spill over into a heavy evaluation and judgmental type of behavior of the
intellectual contributions of the individual
student.  This over-judgmental style can be
very frustrating to a student who has had a
teacher who was considerate and supportive
of his ideas.

Solution:  When student teachers are
anxious they tend to be more evaluative than
necessary.  A student teacher who is attending to individual differences is not as likely
to be judgmental.  Security seems to foster
acceptance.  Find out what is making the
student teacher nervous about the particular
student, class or situation and provide
anxiety reducing alternatives.  Encourage
the student teacher to be an active listener
and not be personally evaluative or judgmental
regarding the pupil problems outside of the
classroom.  Students have a tendency to act
on the advice of the teacher.  Very often
if the teacher is too candid or not specific
enough, the student will act on the student
teacher's advice and this may come back to
trouble the student teacher.

## Why Can't I Wear Blue Jeans?

The fifth problem area is the student
teacher's dress or appearance.  Very often
student teachers will make an effort to look
like the students.  They will dress in whatever the students wear.  They will be reluctant to look like a teacher, although they
want the respect of a teacher.  This is a
very sensitive area with many student teachers.
They resent any suggestion that they shorten
their hair or trim their mustaches up or not
wear blue jeans or student-type clothing.

85

Solution: Often the best way to handle this is to explain to the student teacher that the more a student teacher looks like a teacher, the more a teacher's authority generalizes to the student teacher. Most students behave in a respectful manner toward most teachers. If the student teacher can look like they are part of the teacher group, they will initially command the same kind of respect and behavior from the students. Dressing like a student tends to confuse the students. They may not be entirely sure how they should act toward the "new person". What looks to be a short term strategy for gaining pupil approval may backfire. They find out that they don't command the respect that other teachers in the building do, because they are regarded as a peer. Wearing divergent clothing or student-like apparel, after respect has been established, can be an excellent instruction strategy.

## What Am I Going to Do on Monday?

Student teachers very often are not sure how to make lesson plans. They don't discriminate between instructional objectives and method. They think pages one through forty-four is a lesson plan. Pages one through forty-four may be the instructional objective. The method of instruction may be something quite different.

Solution: If a student is having a problem at the planning level, pointing out that objectives are different from method may help them organize their plan more effectively. Similarly, student teachers very often fail to provide for unplanned events such as shortened class periods. The student teacher should be encouraged to have an alternative lesson plan in mind, in the event that the first plan does not work.

## First Period Went So Well, But Second Period Was Terrible!

The seventh problem area is the non-enthused student teacher. Very often this lack of enthusiasm is related to mood swings that come early in the student teaching experience. The student teacher has had a good day and is exhuberant about his performance. The next day he is less effective, and consequently, less enthused.

Solution: These ups and downs in enthusiasm are quite natural during the first four weeks of student teaching. After four weeks and with the advent of some security, the radical fluctuation in moods should disappear. The student teacher may over react to being ineffective. Help the student teacher realize that these mood swings are very normal and natural.

## You're Just Not Catching On

Another problem area is the overcritical public school supervisor. It is important that the evaluation process be implemented as diagnostic and prescriptive. These two dimensions are the responsibility of the public school supervisor. Simply to evaluate and criticize the student teacher is only going to cause ill feelings and be non-productive. The supervisor is not modeling the kinds of behavior the student teacher will need to be an effective instructor.

Solution: It is important that the student teacher supervisor be a diagnostician. They should be able to situationally explain appropriate and inappropriate behavior and be able to provide the student teacher with some perspective on the kinds of things that will happen to them as they student teach.

## Why Did I Get Stuck With You For A Supervisor?

The public school supervisor may not have had adequate materials or instructional strategies for the student teacher to observe. The student teacher gets increasingly frustrated at the inability of the supervising teacher to model those kinds of behaviors and instructional styles which the student teacher is interested in mastering.

Solution: Explain to all participants that the entire school is at the disposal of the public school supervisor in order to meet the needs of the student teacher. The "solitary craftsman" model of supervising a student teacher is not the most effective model for presenting divergent instructional styles to student teachers. Should another teacher in the building have a particular methodology or a particular style which is effective, it is the public school supervisor's responsibility to let the student teacher experience that particular method of style and consequently, profit from it.

## I'm Afraid to Ask Questions

The biggest threat to good communication is that the student teacher believes that any questions they ask the supervising teacher will reflect a lack of preparation which might be interpreted by the student teacher supervisor as not being motivated. The student teacher may be concerned about the effect all the questions will have on his grade. The student teacher may stop asking questions of the public school supervisor and then begin to make mistakes. The school supervisor may be reluctant to say anything because it might worsen the relationship with the student teacher.

Solution:  The university supervisor
and the building supervisor should be con-
tinuously available to the student teacher.
The student teacher should have problems
answered immediately and questions resolved.
A phone call level communication between the
three participants is very effective.  If a
problem does arise, it can be resolved immediately rather than waiting until the
next day.

**DATE DUE**

| | | | |
|---|---|---|---|
| | | | |
| | | | |
| | | | |
| | | | |
| | | | |
| | | | |
| | | | |
| | | | |
| | | | |
| | | | |
| | | | |
| | | | |
| | | | |
| | | | |
| | | | |
| | | | |

DEMCO 38-297